W9-BYF-755

PHOENIXVILLE PUBLIC LIBRARY
183 SECOND AVENUE
PHOENIXVILLE, PA 19460-3843

WITHDRAWN

XTREME FISH

Marlin

BY S.L. HAMILTON

A&D Xtreme
An imprint of Abdo Publishing | www.abdopublishing.com

Visit us at
www.abdopublishing.com

Published by Abdo Publishing Company, a division of ABDO, PO Box 398166, Minneapolis, Minnesota 55439. Copyright ©2015 by Abdo Consulting Group, Inc. International copyrights reserved in all countries. No part of this book may be reproduced in any form without written permission from the publisher. A&D Xtreme™ is a trademark and logo of Abdo Publishing Company.

Printed in the United States of America, North Mankato, Minnesota.
042014
092014

 PRINTED ON RECYCLED PAPER

Editor: John Hamilton
Graphic Design: Sue Hamilton
Cover Design: Sue Hamilton
Cover Photo: Thinkstock
Interior Photos: Alamy-pgs 6-7; AP-pg 8; Corbis-pgs 9 & 24-25; Dreamstime-pgs 22-23; Getty Images-pgs 1, 4-5, 10-11, 14-15, 16-17, 18-19, 20-21, 26-27 & 29 (inset); Glow Images-pgs 2-3, 12-13, 28-29 & 32; International Game Fish Association-pg 21 (inset); National Oceanic and Atmospheric Administration-pg 18 (inset); RavenFire Media-pg 7 (inset), Wikimedia/AComrade-pg 5 (inset).

Websites
To learn more about Xtreme Fish, visit booklinks.abdopublishing.com. These links are routinely monitored and updated to provide the most current information available.

Library of Congress Control Number: 2014932242

Cataloging-in-Publication Data

Hamilton, S. L.
  Marlin / S. L. Hamilton.
    p. cm. -- (Xtreme fish)
Includes index.
ISBN 978-1-62403-449-7
1. Marlin--Juvenile literature.   2. Marine animals--Juvenile literature.   I. Title.
597--dc23

                                                    2014932242

Contents

Marlin

A marlin is a "billfish." It has a spear-like bill, or snout. These fish are huge, fast, and powerful. They are sometimes called "gladiators of the sea." Marlin are one of the most popular sport fish sought by anglers.

XTREME FACT – The fish's name "marlin" is thought to have originated from a sailor's tool called a marlinspike. The marlin's spiked bill resembles a marlinspike.

A marlinspike

Species & Location

There are 11 species of marlin. All have the spear-like snout. They are often named after their coloration, such as blue, black, white, and striped marlin. Sailfish and spearfish are members of the marlin family.

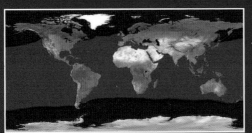

Marlin are found in the Atlantic, Pacific, and Indian Oceans. They swim close to the surface, where the water is usually warmer.

Many marlin species prefer to be far away from land in deep, blue ocean waters. This is why they are often referred to as blue-water fish.

XTREME FACT– Marlin prefer to live by themselves in their own area.

Size

Marlin are so big, they are sometimes referred to as "granders." A "grand" is 1,000 pounds (454 kg). The Atlantic blue marlin is the biggest of the marlin species. It can weigh up to 1,800 pounds (816 kg) and measure up to 16 feet (5 m) in length. Females weigh much more than males. They may be up to four times as heavy.

Author Ernest Hemingway caught a 14-foot (4.3 m) black marlin weighing over one thousand pounds in 1956. Hemingway wrote *The Old Man and the Sea in 1952. It's a story about a fisherman going after a huge marlin.*

Typical marlin sizes today are 50 to 500 pounds (23 to 227 kg). Overfishing for sport and for food has brought a serious decline in the number of monster-sized fish.

In 2008, a blue marlin was caught in the Atlantic Ocean, near Lisbon, Portugal. This European record-breaking marlin weighed 918 pounds (416 kg).

Shape

Marlin are
known for their long
bills, but they are also powerful,
aerodynamically shaped fish. There is
a large dorsal fin on the fish's back. Most
of the time this fin is kept tucked into a
groove in the marlin's body. This keeps the
marlin streamlined, making it easier to
move through the water. When the marlin
wants to herd a school of prey together, it
extends its dorsal fin, which is also called
its "sail."

XTREME FACT– Besides extending its sail (dorsal fin) to herd prey, a marlin may also extend it after eating. Scientists believe this is so the fish can cool down faster.

Bills

A marlin's bill is also called a snout, beak, or rostrum. Many people believe that marlin use their bills to skewer fish onto them like a shish kebab. That happens occasionally when a marlin flips its prey into the air. Usually bills are used to slash into schools of fish. Marlin swim through a group of fish at high speed, slashing left and right. The marlin's slash either stuns, wounds, or kills the prey. The marlin then turns around and swims back to eat the fish floating in the water.

A marlin skewers a dorado fish.

XTREME FACT– Marlin have only small teeth or none at all. They eat their prey whole or in big pieces.

Predator & Prey

Marlin eat fish such as mackerel, tuna, and dolphinfish. They may also dive deep to chew up squid.

Due to their size, speed, and strength, marlin are rarely eaten by other fish. Only huge ocean predators such as great white, mako, and tiger sharks eat marlin. Humans are their greatest threat.

A tiger shark eats a marlin.

Sea lions and a striped marlin compete for a "bait ball" of smaller fish.

XTREME FACT– Marlin fight when attacked. Sharks have been found with marlin bills stuck in their bodies.

Speed

Marlin are super swimmers. They can speed through the ocean at rates of 50 mph (80 kph). However, most of the time marlin float around lazily in warmer water at about 33 feet (10 m) below the surface.

A marlin's slow swimming is believed to be a way of conserving energy. It uses its speed for attacking prey or fleeing from predators.

Blue Marlin

There are two types of blue marlin: Atlantic and Pacific. They are related, but are separate species. They have cobalt blue bodies with white bellies. These fish have the ability to rapidly change color. They have unique pigment and light-reflecting skin cells. When they fight, hunt, or feed, the blue marlin's body appears to light up in a striped pattern.

Atlantic Blue Marlin

Pacific Blue Marlin

XTREME FACT– **All of the largest blue marlin are female. Male marlin rarely grow bigger than 300 pounds (136 kg). According to the International Game Fish Association, the largest Atlantic blue marlin weighed 1,402 pounds (636 kg). The largest Pacific blue marlin weighed 1,376 pounds (624 kg).**

Black Marlin

A black marlin has pectoral fins that stick out from the sides of its body and do not fold flat. This distinguishes it from blue marlin.

A diver examines a black marlin in the Indian Ocean.

A black marlin's body is slate blue, but changes to silver tones when it is feeding or jumping. Because of this, the fish is also known as a silver marlin. It is mainly found in the Pacific and Indian Oceans.

XTREME FACT – The biggest black marlin ever caught weighed 1,560 pounds (708 kg). It was hooked by Alfred C. Glassell, Jr., in the ocean off the village of Cabo Blanco, Peru, South America, in 1953. Today the fish is in the Smithsonian's National Museum of Natural History in Washington, D.C.

White Marlin

White marlin are smaller than other marlin. They are fast swimmers and have a shorter bill. Rather than use the slash-and-stun hunting style, it is believed that they use their fast speed to overtake and eat their prey. They are daytime feeders, using eyesight to find schools of fish.

XTREME FACT– *The largest white marlin on record was 182 pounds (83 kg). It was caught near Vitoria, Brazil, in 1979.*

Although white marlin are actually blue in color, they have a lighter tone and may show some green coloration. They also have light blue or lavender stripes on their sides when they are feeding or jumping.

Striped Marlin

Striped marlin are steely blue, but have blue or lavender vertical stripes on their sides. Unlike other marlin, these stripes remain after the fish has died. Striped marlin have a very long dorsal fin, which runs 90 percent of its body depth.

Striped marlin feed on sardines.

XTREME FACT– *The largest striped marlin on record weighed 494 pounds (224 kg). It was caught off Tutukaka, New Zealand, in 1986.*

The striped marlin lives in the Indian and Pacific Oceans, close to shorelines. It is known as a fighter. Anglers will often say that a hooked striped marlin spends more time in the air than in the water.

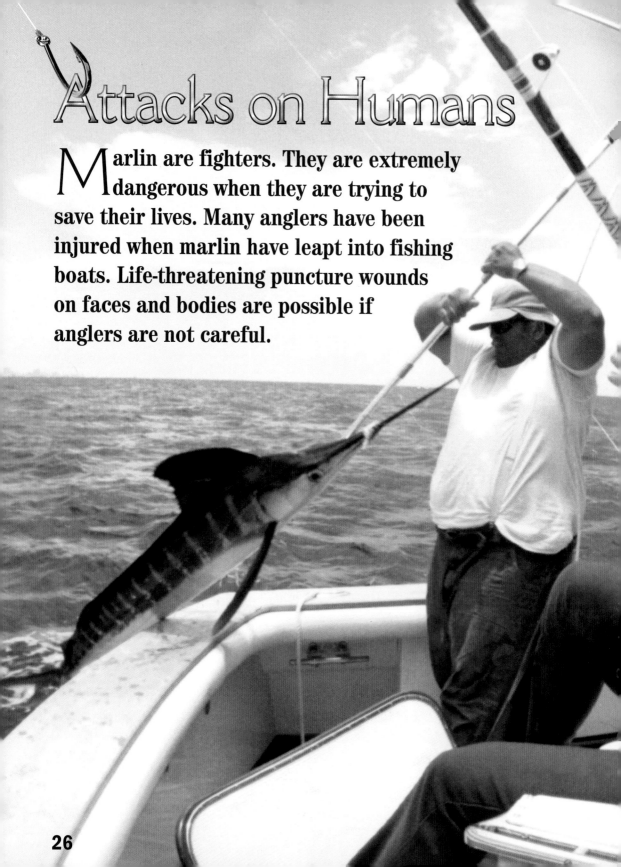

Attacks on Humans

Marlin are fighters. They are extremely dangerous when they are trying to save their lives. Many anglers have been injured when marlin have leapt into fishing boats. Life-threatening puncture wounds on faces and bodies are possible if anglers are not careful.

Fishing for Marlin

When hooked, marlin leap out of the water, twisting, jumping, slashing, and tail-walking. Marlin also "greyhound," making a dozen or more graceful leaps across the water's surface. They will race away, swimming in long runs under the water. It's pure excitement for anglers.

> **XTREME QUOTE** – *"When blue marlin are caught they turn into greyhounds with the strength of a Mack truck and the speed of a rocket."* –*Baja's Awesome Sportfishing Web Site*

Fishermen pose with their marlin catch. For many anglers, landing a marlin is the best fishing experience of their lives.

Glossary

AERODYNAMIC
Something that has a shape that reduces the drag, or resistance, of air or water moving across its surface. Fish with aerodynamic shapes can go faster because they don't have to push as hard to move through the water.

BAIT BALL
When a school of fish swarm into a tight ball in order to protect themselves from predators.

BILLFISH
A large sport fish with a long, pointed bill or snout. Marlin, sailfish, and spearfish are billfish.

BLUE-WATER FISH
Fish that spend their lives far out to sea, living mostly alone. Marlin are blue-water fish.

DORSAL FIN
The fin that is located on the top of a fish's back. On a shark, for example, the dorsal fin is the one that sticks out of the water when the shark is swimming near the surface.

GRANDER
A fish weighing 1,000 pounds (454 kg) or more. A "grand" is a slang term for 1,000.

MARLINSPIKE
A long, pointed metal tool used by sailors to separate strands of rope. It is believed that the marlin fish got its name because its bill looks like this tool.

PECTORAL FIN
Fins found behind a fish's head, on either side of its body.

PREDATOR
An animal that feeds on other animals.

PUNCTURE WOUND
A wound made by an object entering the flesh. The opening in the wound is usually small, but it is often deep. A marlin's bill would make a puncture wound on prey.

SKEWER
To pierce with a long, thin object, such as a metal or wooden stick. Marlin sometimes use their bills to skewer their prey.

SPORT FISH
A type of fish that anglers hunt because of its fierceness and difficulty in landing, making its capture an exciting sport. Marlin are a sport fish.

TAIL-WALK
When a fish appears to "walk" across the surface of the water on its tail.

Index